MORE OF WHAT MATTERS

30 KEYS TO PRODUCTIVITY

J. RANDOLPH TURPIN, JR.

MORE OF WHAT MATTERS

30 KEYS TO PRODUCTIVITY

J. RANDOLPH TURPIN, JR.

DECLARATION PRESS

DECLARATION PRESS

More of What Matters:
30 Keys to Productivity

ISBN-13: 978-0-9983102-4-4

To my father,
Jim Turpin,
who taught me
there's no such word as
"can't."

CONTENTS

INTRODUCTION

Quite often I have been asked, "How do you accomplish so much?" I suppose that people look at the books I have produced and various projects I have going. They know how busy I am, and they wonder how I produce it all, seemingly in a short amount of time.

In the early stages of planning this book, I asked myself, "*Why* am I so productive?" To me, it seems that most of what I do happens automatically. I suppose that comes with decades of practice. I had to really think about it to arrive at an answer to the question. As a result of my reflections, my scribbled notes reminded me that there are a number of acquired attitudes and learned practices I have assimilated into my makeup over the years. After two days of work, I was surprised. There in front of me was a list of thirty keys to productivity that I have found to be personally significant. My purpose here is to share these keys with you, in hope that you will find a few to be helpful in your own development as a productive person.

I am still learning how to be more productive. Observing the methods of other high performers inspires me. Articles and presentations produced by efficiency experts interest me. I find reviews on the latest productivity apps and gadgets fascinating. As a lifetime learner, I will always seek ways to produce more in less time and with fewer resources. I have a lot more to learn, and I am probably more aware of my weaknesses than I am of my strengths.

Awareness of weakness motivates me to improve, and it also helps me to stay in a place of dependence on God. In fact, I can think of a number of areas right now where I am trusting Him for breakthrough. Without Him, I would surely fail, but the good news is that I am not without Him. As the Apostle Paul said to the Philippians, "I can do all things because of Christ who strengthens me" (Philippians 4:13, MEV).

If you see anything worth emulating from my life, I can assure you those patterns and qualities are the result of God's gracious workmanship. There have also been many people who have spurred me on along the way. My parents have probably been the most influential in this area, setting an example of faith and instilling in me a strong work ethic. They and others have contributed to the foundations of who I am. I am grateful.

For me, productivity is all about advancing the influence of Jesus in the world. There is no higher cause. I am on a campaign to empower Christians to serve and lead with excellence, demonstrating God's goodness in every mountain of culture: arts and entertainment; business, science and technology; education; family and family services; government and politics; media and communications; church, religion and spirituality. Although the cliché is overused, I do believe that we are supposed to "make the world a better place." Furthermore, the Lord Jesus *deserves* to be glorified in every realm through our lives of faithfulness and effectiveness.

Do you remember that part of "The Lord's Prayer" that says, "Thy kingdom come. Thy will be done in earth as it is in heaven" (Matthew 6:10, KJV)? Those words are all about bringing the life and culture of heaven into the earth. That kingdom is not just about what *we* get out of this Christian life. It is not just about the benefits *we* receive. There is work for us to do. There are things that we need to accomplish to advance God's purposes in the earth. For this reason, productivity is a topic worthy of our focused consideration.

In the pages that follow, we will review thirty keys to productivity. May the Holy Spirit take my words and plant a few seed-thoughts in your spirit—seed that will produce something beyond my ideas. May you accomplish more than you thought you could. Yes, this book is about *you* producing something for God's glory, but you don't have to do it alone. You are joined to the One who "is able to do exceeding abundantly beyond all that we ask or imagine" (Ephesians 3:20, MEV).

1. Depend on God

D
ependence on God is my number one key to productivity. My words in the Introduction have already pointed in that direction. By relying upon the Lord, I place myself in a posture of humility, and wherever there is humility, there God delights in giving His empowering and enabling grace. The Bible tells us in more than one place that God gives grace to the humble (Psalm 138:4; Proverbs 3:34; James 4:6; 1 Peter 5:5).

By relying or depending on God, I gain access to all that He is and all that He has provided for my success. Actually, He is more committed to my success than I am. Productivity in the kingdom of heaven is rooted in dependence upon God.

I am reminded today of John 15:4-5 (NIV)—a passage that relates to this virtuous attitude of dependence. Here Jesus instructed His disciples, saying,

> Remain in me, as I also remain in you. No branch can bear fruit by itself; it must remain in the vine. Neither can you bear fruit unless you remain in me. I am the vine; you are the branches. If you remain in me and I in you, you will bear much fruit; apart from me you can do nothing.

Jesus said, "Apart from me, you can do nothing." These words can also be translated, "Apart from me, you can *produce* nothing." So true. I am keenly aware of my need for the Lord. Apart from Him, I am ineffective. If Jesus is not at the center of my life, and if I neglect my relationship with Him, I can produce nothing of eternal worth.

It is true that apart from Jesus, I can produce nothing, but the good news is that I am *not* apart from Him. Because my life is integrated with His, I have the potential to produce fruit that is consistent with His character. Before my life became established in Christ, I was limited to the weakness of my flesh, but now, because of my dependence on Him, "I can do all things because of Christ who strengthens me" (Philippians 4:13, MEV).

Our dependence on God is more than a mere default mode that we fall into when we don't know what else to do. We intentionally rely on Him. We make a choice to focus on an intimate relationship with God, and that intimacy is a key to productivity for anyone serving in Christ's kingdom. That choice surfaces every time we pray, worship, meditate on Scripture and spend time in God's presence. Our accomplishments will rise out of our intentional choice to sustain that heart-to-heart connection.

2. Do What Father Is Doing

Jesus is our example in everything, even productivity. We have already considered His emphasis on how *we* can produce nothing apart from Him, but are you aware of the fact that *Jesus* could produce nothing apart from His fellowship with His Father? Consider what He said in John 5:19 (NIV):

> Jesus gave them this answer: "Very truly I tell you, the Son can do nothing by himself; he can do only what he sees his Father doing, because whatever the Father does the Son also does."

Jesus said, "The Son can do nothing by Himself." Those words remind us of what we have already heard in John 15: "Apart from me, you can do nothing." In John 15, Jesus was talking *to His disciples,* but in John 5, He was talking *about Himself.*

It is understandable that Jesus' disciples had to depend on Him. They were mere humans, and obviously, they needed Jesus. But Jesus said regarding Himself, "the Son can do nothing by Himself; He can do only what He sees His Father doing."

So, here is God in the flesh declaring His dependence—His dependence on His Father. Remember that Jesus came as both God and man. As a human, He could have acted entirely on His own, but He chose not to. He did not come to do His own will. In order to fulfill heaven's purposes, Jesus was dependent on perceiving what His Father was doing. Whatever the Father did, that is what the Son did.

From Jesus' words in John 5:19, we can discern three features of His productive life:

1. **Dependence.** The Son can do nothing by Himself.

2. **Perception.** The Son was able to perceive what the Father was doing.

3. **Alignment and Obedience.** Whatever the Father was doing, that was precisely what the Son did.

Jesus did not randomly go from place to place performing His mighty works. He moved about purposefully, and He ministered with precision. That precision was the result of perceiving His Father's actions and aligning Himself accordingly. If that was the way that Jesus conducted Himself, how much more so do we need to do the same. His pattern is the example for us to follow.

Perception of Father's Actions

In the conduct of His life and ministry, Jesus relied upon His *perception* of what His Father was doing. We also need that awareness of the Father's intentions. Awareness is in part the result of watching and listening. Jesus taught His disciples to take heed of what they heard (Mark 4:24; Luke 8:18). "Take heed" is an old expression somewhat synonymous to "pay attention" or "listen and follow." When we take heed, we carefully consider what is communicated to us. We place a high value on what is said or shown because we fully intend to align our attitudes, beliefs and actions with that instruction. When we take heed, we are not just listening; we are *truly* listening—listening *and* obeying.

We have a real relationship with God the Father, and like any good relationship, it includes communication. I do believe God speaks to us when we ask questions like, "Father, what are you doing today?" He does communicate wisdom to us when we ask Him for it. He promised that He would answer in such a way in James 1:5 (NIV):

> If any of you lacks wisdom, you should ask God, who
> gives generously to all without finding fault, and it
> will be given to you.

That wisdom may come as a thought or as a hunch. It may come as a sudden sense of knowing or through a perspective not previously considered.

Most of what we need to know about our Father's will is already detailed in the pages of the Holy Bible. Search out His revealed desires and purposes. Study His Word. Listen for His voice. Once you have heard what you believe to be His voice, put it to the test. Try responding to that voice. Step out in obedience. The best way to grow in your ability to recognize God's voice is to obey what you are already hearing. Be a good steward of a few things, and trust that your faithfulness will result in Father entrusting to you more. You always have the opportunity to check it out with the Bible to make sure what you are hearing is consistent with God's established ways of working. Experience and practice will help you to recognize God's voice when it is truly Him talking.

Cultivate the hearing of His voice. Aim to sharpen your awareness of what He is saying and doing. It begins with a *desire* to recognize your Father's voice. Ask Him to speak. Then pay attention to the streams of thought that run through your mind and spirit. Those thoughts might just be God's thoughts.

Alignment with Father's Actions

Once you have perceived the Father's actions and intentions, align yourself with what He is doing. What we are considering here is a pathway to *precision* in life, accomplishing things that are worth accomplishing, rather than living randomly or guessing our way through decisions. Steer away from a "shotgun" approach to your endeavors, hoping that at least one of your random efforts hits a significant target. Aim to be a sharpshooter. Increased productivity and precision are more likely to occur when you start the day asking, "Father, what are you doing today? I want to align my thoughts, my commitments and my actions with what you are doing." Once you ask, pay attention to how He responds.

Years ago, I heard someone say, "Rather than ask God to bless what you are doing, find out what God is blessing, and then do *that* thing." Do you realize that when you do this, you are partnering with the Creator? Do you realize that when you make this your practice, you are entering into a realm of *supernatural productivity*?

Think of it this way: you are becoming yoked together with Jesus! Rather than working *for* Jesus, you are working *with* Jesus! Be attentive to what God is doing, and then do what He is doing. I have held onto this philosophy for nearly thirty years. Life is a lot easier when you are yoked with Jesus and what He has already willed to do in a situation. When we place our hand with God's hand on a task, we cannot help but succeed.

Get close to the heart of our Father. Out of that place near His heart, you will have the ability to perceive what He is doing and what He desires. It is then that you will be positioned to align your actions with His and experience great kingdom success.

3. DO WHAT IS RIGHT

Father is always doing the right thing; therefore, when I align with Him and do what He is doing, *I* am doing the right thing. We are talking about living according to the clearly defined ways of righteousness. It is called obedience.

Obedience is always right. At times, it may appear easier to take shortcuts, to do what is convenient, or to do what will bring you the greatest immediate benefits. However, doing what pleases the Lord is the ultimate achievement. After all, true success can only be measured in terms of the degree to which we have been faithful and effective in matters of God's will.

I have found that when people function in a way that is not truly right, they start making mistakes and end up in a place of regret. Their work ultimately proves to be inferior, and it certainly does not bring glory to God. Typically, such errors become costly, and everyone involved has to go back to the "drawing board" and start all over. Eventually, like it or not, they will have to do it the right way anyway. Why not do it right from the very beginning?

Always take care to do the right thing *the right way*. What I particularly have in mind is the need to consider how our actions affect other people. Even if we think that we can justify an action on the basis of Scripture, it can still be the wrong thing to do if we have no regard for those who might be negatively impacted by what we do. A dilemma of this sort is rare, but it does sometimes happen. Thankfully, godly wisdom will guide us so that our actions will be honorable toward the people involved.

Discern what is right, and do what is right. Whenever the will of God is perceived, be prompt and thorough in your obedience. Do not delay, and do not modify His instructions. If further wisdom is needed, ask Him for it. He loves to give it, because Father God delights in seeing His ways lived out in the earth.

4. PRAY AND PROPHESY

E vidence of Jesus' dependence on His Father is seen in His lifestyle of prayerfulness. He spent much time alone in His Father's presence. Then He would come out of those prayer times ministering with great effectiveness. Then back into prayer He went. As someone has rightly said, "Jesus ministered between places of prayer."

Jesus' disciples observed His pattern. They saw how Jesus would go into the presence of His Father, petitioning Him for the will of heaven to be done in the earth. They saw Him come out of those prayer times in great power, manifesting supernatural results by prophetically speaking and acting in the midst of impossible situations. Then He would return to solitary communion with His Father.

"We want to be like that," they must have thought to themselves. I suggest that they *did* think this way because of what we know about what they said on one occasion. After observing Jesus in a time of prayer, they said to Him, "Lord, teach us to pray" (Luke 11:1, NIV).

In a few moments, I will show you how Jesus responded to their request, but first I want to address this question: "Why pray?" Stated another way, "Since God is sovereign, does prayer make any difference? He is God, so, won't He ultimately do whatever *He* wants to do, with or without us praying?" The simple answer is "No, God will not do whatever He wants, without us praying." God has chosen to work through us, not apart from us.

When Jesus' disciples said, "Lord, teach us to pray," His response shows us that prayer is the means by which God gets things done in the earth. In Luke 11:2 (NIV), Jesus taught us to pray,

> "Our Father, who is in heaven,
> hallowed be Your name.
> Your kingdom come;
> Your will be done on earth, as it is in heaven."

God does not just decide to do things and then step forward to do them. Rather, here is how He works. Men and women like you and me enter the presence of God, and while we are there in His presence, we discern and pray heaven's will. Like Jesus, we petition the Father for His kingdom to come and for His will to be done on earth as it is in heaven. Then when we step out of our prayer closets, we confront the matters of life, and as we do, we prophetically speak and act on the revealed will of heaven, to make it a reality in the earth.

Now, let's apply what we are learning to our work. Pray about your work. Ask Father about the specifics. Get His wisdom—His will that has already been established in heaven. Once you have discerned the heart and mind of heaven, take action accordingly—even to the point of making prophetic declarations over the forward movement that is needed.

In my opinion, the people of God should be the most productive and most successful people on the planet. Look at us! We are the sons and daughters of God! We are filled with the same Spirit that raised Jesus from the dead! We have access to the throne room of heaven, where all of the wisdom and resource we will ever need has been made available!

People who are highly productive in heaven's purposes typically live from a place of God's presence. They steward His presence in their lives, and they cultivate intimacy and dependency with the Lord. They are men and women of prayer, and once they have touched heaven, they courageously become the prophetic conduit through which heaven touches earth.

5. Stay True to Your Mission

What is your mission? What is your life vision? You need to know why you are doing what you are doing. I have found that knowing my life mission and vision is a key to consistently producing what really matters.

In the early days of my ministry, I remember being asked this question by the ministerial credentialing board: "What is your vision for your ministry?" I was young in pastoral work, and at that point, I did not have a clue where my calling was taking me as far as the big picture of life was concerned. I think I responded something like this: "My vision is to preach a good sermon next Sunday!" I could not see any further than the next church service!

It is okay if you cannot totally explain your *personal* mission and vision, but I would encourage you to begin asking God for wisdom and insight into *His* mission and vision. There are aspects of the Christian mission that belong to all of us. For instance, we all share the common mission of taking the gospel to the world. We share the common mission of loving God and loving people.

You also have a unique, personal mission within that broader, general mission. Over time, reoccurring themes and passions surface in your life. Pull out your journal, turn to a blank page, and write them down. These serve as indicators of your unique role.

I am currently in a phase of life that some call "The Third Act." In my earliest years, others contributed to my formation. Then out of the person I had become, I worked, served and produced. Now, I am occupied with contributing to the formation of others, just as others were instrumental in my development in my earliest years. In this phase, I have articulated my mission in these words: "My mission is to empower the rising generation for cultural transformation and spiritual awakening."

What is your mission? Now, don't take my mission and try to make it yours. Those words are the result of sixty years of living. That statement has taken shape over time. I am only giving it to you as an example. Yours might end up being something similar to what I have written, but be sure to prayerfully think through what your life mission is, and keep it in front of you.

I live every day with my mission in front of me. Whatever I have done today has been for the purpose of empowering the rising generation for cultural transformation and spiritual awakening. For me, that begins with my family. My number one responsibility with my children and grandchildren is to empower them for cultural transformation and spiritual awakening. I am in a situation right now where I have intentionally made my family the priority as it relates to my life mission. I am giving this matter my best efforts and my intentional focus.

Keep your mission in the forefront of your mind. It would be helpful to write it down, display it, and speak of it frequently. Your awareness of mission will be your guide as you set priorities. Things that do not line up with that mission should probably be discarded. They are distractions. I try not to invest myself into things that do not relate to my mission. If it does not have something to do with cultural transformation or spiritual awakening, I'll probably not give myself to it.

6. DEFINE SUCCESS AND AIM FOR IT

How will you know that you are succeeding in your mission? What is success to you? As far as I am concerned, I cannot define what success is without first considering what is success in the eyes of our Father. To me, success is "being faithful and effective in whatever God requires of me." I have to look at what I am doing and measure it in those terms. If you are also a person who chooses to measure success in terms of what God requires, I have a few additional thoughts to share in this regard.

Obviously, this approach to defining success involves discerning the specifics of our Father's requirements. The Bible contains plenty of indicators revealing His expectations of *all* people. Knowing God's will in a broad sense—His expectations of *all*—most often leads to the discernment of what we need to individually accomplish.

There is a *unique* purpose and mission for your life. What has He required of you? What is His calling upon your life? If you cannot answer these questions with absolute certainty, what would you *hope* that His calling might be? The answer to that last question may be closer to the truth than you have imagined.

Once you have gained a sense of what God is requiring, what would be the indicators showing you that you are faithfully and effectively fulfilling that end? From a productivity point of view, these indicators might be your measures of success.

Not only are we to define what success means for our overall life, but each project or task also needs its definition of success. This defining process begins with assessing what needs to be done. On the basis of that assessment, goals should be set. Then we need to think through how we will know when those goals have been reached. In other words, what will be in the indicators of success?

A word of caution is in order. Keep in mind that we are talking about success as it relates to productivity. We are not talking about your identity, your spiritual standing or your acceptance in your Father's eyes. Your performance will not make your Father love you any more or any less.

My performance does not affect His love for me; however, His love does empower me to live a productive life. I love Him because He first loved me. This Father-child love relationship is motivation enough for me to give my best toward the fulfillment of my personal life mission.

7. FOCUS

Focus. Your focus will determine your direction, and it will affect the outcome of your endeavors. Focus will determine what will increase. What you focus on has a tendency to grow. Over time, you will get more of what you have become fixated on. This truth is both a sobering and liberating realization.

Focus on What Matters

When I was a teenager and started getting serious about my walk with the Lord, I said to Him, "Lord, I only want to devote my life to matters of eternal significance. I do not want to devote my life to pursuits that terminate in this life. I want to give myself to eternal things."

A good way to assess whether or not you are giving yourself to eternal matters is to ask this question: "What difference will this task, project or pursuit make ten thousand years from now?" I could ask, "What difference will it make in eternity?" but we cannot comprehend the concept of eternity. It is too vast for us, but maybe we *can* comprehend the concept of ten thousand years. To think of it another way, we could ask, "What impact will this action or pursuit have on the lives of others in the generations that follow me? How will they be affected by my obedience and follow-through?"

What matters the most? Not everything is equally worthy of my time, attention and resources. There are some matters in life that others can address; I do not have to be the one to go after those things. There are other matters that only I can address. For instance, only I can be a husband to my wife. Only I can be a father to my children. Only I can be a grandfather to my grandchildren. Only I can live my life of devotion to God. Others could take care of much within the realm of my concern, but there are a few things that only I can do. Those items are priority with me.

Now zoom in on your responsibilities in work and leadership. Ask the same question. What matters most in your company, organization or ministry? What matters most in your current project? What will matter the most in the next eight hours? What matters most in the current problem or task you are trying to work through? How will you define what matters most to you? Once you have identified what really matters, stay focused on those things.

Focus on One Thing

Multitasking is nearly impossible. In my informed opinion, it is time for humanity to recognize and admit that this thing called multitasking defies reason and is not as virtuous as we have been led to believe. People can only effectively focus on one thing at a time. The only exception would be mothers of small children. They alone have an amazing ability to deal with crying children while talking on the phone, preparing dinner, ironing clothes and keeping their composure at the same time.

We live in a time when companies are downsizing. As a result, both the employee and the executive are expected to wear multiple hats. The number of tasks and projects that each person has to take on is ridiculous. When I am in environments like that, let me tell you what it feels like inside of my brain. I feel like I am standing in the entertainment department of Target or Walmart, and every television on that back wall is turned on to a different channel with the volume turned up full blast. It is an overload, and the possibility of anything productive occurring in that situation is minimal if not nonexistent. If I do not have the power to change the situation, I have to back away until I can gain an internal focus. If I don't do that, I will shut down and become useless to that organization.

Many job descriptions read, "Must be good at multitasking," but work environments insisting on making multitasking normative are generally inefficient. Others may disagree with me on this point, but having served as a supervisor and employee in a number of organizations requiring a high level of productivity, I have found that people work best when they are allowed to focus on one major project at a time.

Focus on one thing at a time. When you get up in the morning, ask yourself this question: "What one thing can I do today to advance in my mission? What will help me feel like I have succeeded in my work today?" Before you leave that board or committee meeting, ask yourself, "What one thing can I do in the next ten minutes that will advance what we just discussed in that meeting?" While conversing with a group of people, ask yourself, "What one thing can I say in this conversation that will move matters in a productive and redemptive direction?" Stay focused on one thing at a time.

8. Discern Between
Urgent and Important

Train yourself to discern between the urgent and the important. Learning to make this distinction is integral to gaining the needed focus emphasized in the previous chapter. I almost included the *urgent versus important* dynamic in that section, but I have placed it here to elevate its importance. Consider this chapter, "Focus, Part Two."

Most of us probably live and serve in unfocused environments where many things claim to be urgent and important. Given that reality, how does a person decide what their focus will be? In his book, *The 7 Habits of Highly Effective People,* Stephen R. Covey popularized the Eisenhower Decision Matrix. This matrix offers a helpful filter. When trying to gain your focus, consider these four categories of decision-making:

1. Important and Urgent

2. Unimportant and Urgent

3. Important and Not Urgent

4. Unimportant and Not Urgent

In which of these areas would you *prefer* to focus? Most of us would probably choose "Important and Not

Urgent," because that is where our most creative and significant efforts can take place. Avoid "Unimportant and Not Urgent" as much as possible. If your superiors require it, diligently work through the "Unimportant and Urgent" tasks, but then get away from them as quickly as you can. In a given day, the "Important and Urgent" should be your priority. However, the ideal is to live most of your life in the "Important and Not Urgent."

The Tyranny of the Urgent

Many things may come your way with the *appearance* of urgency, but they are not equally important. I am sure you have heard of "the tyranny of the urgent"—an expression popularized by Charles E. Hummel. That is what we want to avoid. Life, ministry and work should not consist entirely of crisis after crisis after crisis. Take care to cultivate a culture where crises and urgent matters are not allowed to rule the environment or set the agenda for your life and work.

If you are in doubt concerning the urgency of a matter, as long as someone is not in immediate danger, it may be best to wait before acting. If something claims to be urgent, and if I do not have clarity on how to proceed, I typically hold until clarity comes. I may not have to wait for more than five or ten minutes, but I do wait to see what wisdom the Lord might give. If I do not receive confirmation that it is an urgent situation, I won't totally ignore the matter, yet at the same time, I will not allow it to consume me. Now, do not construe what I am saying here as a license for indecisiveness. Sometimes any decision is better than no decision at all. Be discerning.

Choose Your Battles

Not everything needs to be given priority attention. Even troubling matters may not warrant immediate action. Some things can wait. Pray, and wait to see what God does. He may give you the wisdom to take a positive action to offset the negative matter. As a result, the need for a frontal assault on the negative situation may be eliminated.

Choose your battles. The battle is the Lord's anyway, isn't it? A number of years ago, the Lord said to me, "Randy, there are some battles that I never intended for you to fight." There are times we just need to stand still and watch the Lord win the victory.

Be careful here. Some could take my point and act irresponsibly. Do not neglect things you should not be neglecting. The real reason for addressing this issue of urgency is to raise the awareness of how seemingly urgent matters can distract from the needed focus on things that are truly important.

9. ELEVATE PEOPLE OVER PAPER

Elevate *people* over *paper*. What do I mean by "people over paper"? I am using the word "paper" as a metaphor to represent administration, projects and tasks—that stack of papers piling up on your desk. I am using the word "people" to mean the actual living and breathing people around you.

But There is Work to Do

While everyone believes that people are important, in demanding work environments, the prevailing attitude can become one that says, "Yes, people are important, but there is work to do! How can we possibly find time to invest into one another?" I understand the dilemma, but let us consider how making human beings a priority actually increases productivity.

There is a tension between being people-oriented and being task-oriented (i.e., paper-oriented). Some people are very good at tasks, but they may not be very strong with people skills. Others are good with people skills, but they may not be good at organizing and administering tasks. Then there are some who may be like me. I think that I live in a healthy tension between the two—between being people-oriented and being task-oriented. However, I truly believe we ultimately need to elevate people over paper. In so doing, we will more faithfully reflect the heart of God, and we will actually accomplish more. I will explain how this elevation of the human factor impacts productivity.

I may have a list of things I have got to do in a given day. For example, I might have ten things on my to-do list. I could devote my entire day to working through that list, and in a best-case scenario, I might complete most of those items. However, if I were to devote my priority time to strategically connecting with people in my organization or network, greater productivity can result.

Why might that be true? If we elevate people, making them the priority, in that interpersonal connection, we exchange essential information, we affirm their value, we boost morale, we invest into their lives, we spur them on, and we ignite a synergy that will lead to greater creativity and innovation.

Through people-connections, we equip, empower and release the total workforce to accomplish much more than any of us as individuals can accomplish. If I make time with people a priority, not only will I still do some of the things on my list, but I will also empower them to do what God is requiring of them. If I am empowering other people, I am activating them to get more work done than I could ever do by myself. I can also recruit some of them to be hands-on in my area of responsibility, assisting with a few of the projects or tasks that I have got to address.

Empowering people is not just about delegation. Delegation is an incidental aspect of empowerment. I am talking about *truly* valuing individuals and setting them up for success. When I demonstrate to them that I value them, I am facilitating the possibility that they could make a major kingdom impact at some point in their day.

By elevating people over paper, I actually become more effective in what I am there to do. I am *committed* to elevating people, and it is something I have to be *intentional* about. I find that I accomplish a lot more when I invest into people in this way because I cannot do everything required of me based on my skills, experience and resources alone.

The Power of "One Another"

Value the role that other people play in your life. I find that much is accomplished in my life through collaboration with others—working with teams of people. In fact, I would say that the greater matters of life and destiny are accomplished in community. God did not create you to succeed alone. Do not try to accomplish everything all by yourself. God has given you other people in this world to assist you.

You have gifts that are beneficial to others. Others have gifts in them that are beneficial to you. None of us alone have everything that we need. We need one another. The New Testament has an abundance of teaching about the life we are to live in relationship with one another. Study it out. There is a huge list of "one another" teachings in the Bible. Here are just a few of them:

1. Live in harmony and peace with each other (Mark 9:50; Romans 12:16; 1 Peter 3:8).

2. Love one another (John 13:34, 35; 15:12, 17; Romans 13:8; 1 Thessalonians 4:9; 1 Peter 3:8; 4:8; 1 John 3:11, 23; 4:7, 11, 12; 2 John 5).

3. Be devoted to one another in brotherly love (Romans 12:10).

4. Honor one another above yourselves (Romans 12:10).

5. Stop passing judgment on one another (Romans 14:13).

6. Accept one another just as Christ accepted you (Romans 15:7)

7. Instruct one another (Romans 15:14).

8. When you come together to eat, wait for each other (1 Corinthians 11:33).

9. Have equal concern for each other (1 Corinthians 12:25).

10. Serve one another in love (Galatians 5:13).

11. Carry each other's burdens (Galatians 6:2).

12. Be patient, bearing with one another in love (Ephesians 4:2; Colossians 3:13).

13. Be kind and compassionate to one another (Ephesians 4:32).

14. Submit to one another out of reverence for Christ (Ephesians 5:21).

15. In humility, consider others better than yourselves (Philippians 2:3; 1 Peter 5:5).

16. Forgive whatever grievances you may have against one another (Colossians 3:13).

17. Admonish one another (Colossians 3:16).

18. Make your love increase and overflow for each other (1 Thessalonians 3:12).

19. Encourage each other (1 Thessalonians 4:18; 5:11; Hebrews 3:13; 10:25).

20. Build each other up (1 Thessalonians 5:11).

21. Spur one another on toward love and good deeds (Hebrews 10:24).

22. Confess your sins to each other, and pray for each other, that you may be healed (James 5:16).

23. Offer hospitality to one another without grumbling (1 Peter 4:9).

24. Each one should use whatever gift he has received to serve others (1 Peter 4:10).

Meditate on those passages. Apply them, and you will discover the value of community. Isolation is not healthy. The moment you become isolated, you run the risk of giving your best energies to things that are not going to amount to much. Be a good steward of relationships. Make people a priority.

10. STAY POSITIVE

Stay positive. "Oh, but we have to keep in touch with reality, even if it is negative" someone may object. Listen, I have found that negativity accomplishes nothing, and a positive attitude is much closer to reality—the truth that God intended us to live. Think victoriously, live confidently, and associate with other people who think and live the same way.

Think Victoriously

Thoughts of defeat are not to linger in your brain. Think victoriously. Believe that God is who He says He is. Believe that you are who God says you are. Believe that you can do what He says you can do! As my father, Jim Turpin, used to say, *"There is no such word as 'can't'!"*

Get your hopes up! Hope is an indispensable component in the victorious mindset. Hope is not the uncertain and doubtful "I hope so" attitude that we sometimes encounter. It is a lot more positive than that. Hope is the confident expectation of a favorable outcome.

Let's go a little deeper with the concept of hope. Steve Backlund, the founder of Igniting Hope Ministries, is famous for saying, "Our hopelessness about a problem is a bigger problem than the problem." He and Francis

Frangipane have both rightly noted that the absence of "glistening hope" is evidence that we are believing a lie in some area of our life. A key to victorious thinking is to identify the lies we are believing and replace those lies with truth.

The Bible teaches that we are transformed by the renewing of our minds (Romans 12:2). To renew our minds, we need to take heed to the truth of God's Word. Seek out that truth. Meditate on it. Believe it. Act on it, and make it your confession.

The confession of your mouth will determine your direction. The Bible tells us that the tongue is like the rudder of a ship (James 3:4-5). Just as a rudder steers the direction of a ship, so the tongue steers the direction of a person's life. If you want to know what direction your life is taking, listen to how you are talking. When you speak a thing, the mind goes to work reinforcing what you have said, aligning other supporting thoughts with it. Through the repeated speaking of a matter, we establish mindsets, and with established mindsets, the course of life is determined. May the speaking of liberating truth be the characteristic sound on our lips.

Live Confidently

Live with confidence. At its root, the word "confidence" means "with trust." In some contexts, it is synonymous with courage. Live your life with confidence that the matters you are addressing are worthy of your best efforts. Trust that with God's help, you are capable to complete the work at hand. Take courage, for He is with you to provide the needed strength, wisdom, resource and favor. Keep your chin up, put a smile on your face, look straight through all obstacles like an unstoppable man or woman on a mission, and go for it as though failure is an impossibility.

Associate with Positive People

Life requires us to interact with people of every temperament. Because we are on this planet to make a redemptive difference, we must even touch the lives of those who are not as positive or emotionally healthy as we would like them to be. I am talking about individuals who drain us a bit. If *we* are emotionally healthy, we should not totally avoid them. They are often the very hurting people to whom we are supposed to minister.

However, it is not wise to allow negative people into our *inner circle* of relationships. Constant and close association with negativism will deplete us. Yes, we are supposed to minister to those who are weak and unhealthy, but how can we faithfully serve them, if *we* have become empty, fatigued and discouraged? We cannot. It is largely for the good of the hurting ones that we must guard our inner circle.

Your inner circle should consist of carefully selected, like-minded peers. These individuals are not rivals competing for attention or the lead role in the organization. They are not pessimists or chronic complainers. These are positive, life-giving people. These are the people who are going to encourage you and help you fulfill your mission. A mutual exchange is needed with this group; at times, you will impart to them, and at other times, they will impart to you. These are the people to whom you want to give your best energies. They hold to the same values that you regard; therefore, they are worthy of your focused attention. Healthy inner-circle relationships will position you to better serve people who are outside of that circle.

I try to include in my inner circle prophetic, victorious mindset individuals who value what I value. These are people who reverence the presence of God and pay attention to His voice. Here is what happens when I am with these friends. If I start getting off course a little, they have the freedom to say to me, "Randy, are you sure that's what Father is doing in this situation?" They help to keep me in check. There's some accountability there.

You can see why I would not want to make myself open and vulnerable to individuals who do not value the voice of God and kingdom priorities. I associate with people who share the same priorities. I am not saying those are the only people with whom I am connected, but I am talking about my inner circle. If you're asking me how I am able to accomplish so much of what really matters, this is definitely one of the keys. I am careful about my close associations.

Everybody needs friends with whom they can be themselves. Here in this circle is where your "presentation persona" gets put aside. Here you are among the people you can trust. They have got your back. Few can fit into this circle, and negative people certainly do not belong there.

11. DEFINE AND ENFORCE BOUNDARIES

Define and enforce your boundaries. Boundaries are the lines that we draw to limit and define what we will and will not allow. To sustain a high level of productivity, I have to set boundaries in the areas of time, space, resources and even behavior.

Yes and No

Learn to inform others of your boundaries, and be ready to respectfully defend those boundaries. One aspect of this key is knowing when to say "yes" and when to say "no." Recently I heard someone say that highly productive people say "no" a lot more than they say "yes," and I believe that to be true. If I keep saying "yes" to the things that I should be saying "no" to, then when the time comes when I should be saying "yes," I will have nothing left to give to that matter. I will find myself saying "no" to something that would have otherwise been worthwhile.

The Servant Question

But aren't we supposed to be servants? Aren't we supposed to be living sacrificially? Aren't we supposed to be laying our lives down for others? Isn't Christian ministry leadership all about putting others ahead of ourselves? The servant question is an important question.

I have devoted most of my professional life to Christian ministry leadership. As a Christian, I am committed to a lifestyle of laying myself down for the good of others. I aim to prefer others over myself. I would rather give than receive. But here is the problem. If others keep trespassing into sacred space, the emotional drain impairs my ability to authentically open my life to others in love. I want to be accessible, but unregulated accessibility eventually results in me having nothing worth accessing. I am left with little to give. If others keep *taking*, I have nothing left to *voluntarily offer*.

Clarifying Misconceptions

This matter of setting boundaries is one area that others often misunderstand. Some get offended when you talk about boundaries. They think that you are being aloof or that you do not want to spend time with them. Such offense usually occurs when either the leader has not clearly communicated his or her limits, or the offended person simply does not understand the concept of boundaries. In either case, a little improvement in communication on the part of the leader may be helpful.

12. Take Charge of Your Time

Take charge of your time. If you don't take charge of it, somebody else or something else will try to take charge of it for you. Plan ahead of everyone else. Plan ahead of anticipated demands. It is important to always have a project management plan in motion. The moment that you have a void in your schedule, someone else's agenda will get sucked into that vacuum. I might be overstating the point, but I am doing so to make the point.

We used to call this "time management." Actually, a person cannot manage time. Rather, we are stewards of the affairs of life that fit within the time we are given. We all have the same amount of time. You have the same amount as the President of the United States or the Queen of England. Although some physicists may disagree, for our purposes, time is a constant, and it will tick away at the same pace no matter who you are and no matter what you tell it to do.

Three Thirds

Let me get real practical here. I'll show you how I manage the affairs of a given day. I like to take my day and divide it into three thirds: morning, afternoon and evening. My aim is to devote two of those thirds to my work, business or ministry and one of those thirds to personal time. Personal time can include rest, recreation, family time or anything else of a non-work, personal nature. If I have to work in the morning and work in the afternoon, generally I will make sure that the evening— that final third—is reserved for my personal time. If I see that I have got to work in the afternoon and evening, I will reserve the morning for personal time. If I must work in the morning and evening, the afternoon becomes my personal time. Whatever block of time I have designated as personal time, that becomes a *solid commitment* for me. Unless it is a real emergency, nothing is allowed to interfere. If someone asks if I am available to meet at that time, my answer is "no."

If you do not devise a system of some sort, you risk creating fatigue for you, your family and the people that love you. The people close to you need you in their life. Your family needs you. You might feel that you are fine working twenty-four-seven for a while, but it will wear your family out more quickly than it will wear you out.

If you keep a written or digital schedule that others access—such as a shared calendar, do not label your personal time as "time off," "vacation" or "personal time." Others can look at that and say, "Look at all of the time this guy is taking off!" I typically note my personal time with this abbreviation: "FLE." Usually, no one will question it, but if they do ask what "FLE" is, I tell them, "It's a Family Life Event." You may prefer to use some other abbreviation or acronym to protect these sacred blocks of time from the criticisms of the uninitiated. I credit Dr. Lamar Vest for this idea.

Unless it is your supervisor, don't let other people dictate your time and space. I do understand that some of you are not in control of your work situation. You may be dependent every day on bosses dictating your priorities. I understand that. In that case, your employer's list of priorities becomes your list of priorities, but hopefully, you will still have some input to help make your workplace a healthy environment. If so, respectfully express your sense of priorities pertaining to your work.

Adrenaline Addiction

If you are a highly motivated, self-starting kind of person, there will be times when you will be driven by sheer adrenaline. If you are overworking in Christian ministry, you need to realize that what is sometimes thought to be a "divine anointing" for non-stop work is actually nothing more than adrenaline. It's not anointing; it is adrenaline. And adrenaline can become addictive because of the rush that you feel after going two or three days without sleep. I am not kidding. Believe me; I have been there. Others may praise you for your sacrifice, but it is not a healthy thing, and it is not virtuous.

Prioritizing Your Task List

We have addressed how to divide your workday; now let's talk about prioritizing your task list. First, I have to say that a person can overdo a task list approach to their work. If you are not careful, you can put too many things on that list. If you have listed thirty items, and you have only accomplished five of them, those twenty-five untouched tasks are still staring you in the face. Even though you have five completed items that you could be celebrating, you are left feeling overwhelmed.

What could be done differently? First, that list of thirty tasks is too long. Second, there are some good ways to prioritize work into categories. I like to divide my priority list into three categories:

1. Must. These are the tasks that I *must* do. The "must" items are the immediate tasks that keep the organization moving forward. If I do not do these things, there are negative repercussions.

2. Should. These are the tasks that I *should* do. The "should" items are the things that will keep the organization at a healthy level of operation. If all I do are the "must" items, I am living my life according to the tyranny of the urgent. By giving attention to "should" tasks, I preclude problems. I am activating systems and fulfilling other tasks that will prevent potential problems from occurring. I am doing preventative things, minimizing the future necessity for remedial actions. By devoting myself to the "should" category, I build foundations, create environments and establish culture.

3. Want. These are the tasks that I *want* to do. Some might think we don't have time for the "wants." Even the label on the category makes it sound like unnecessary fluff. On the contrary, for productive, visionary people, "want" pursuits are essential to forward movement. A "want" task is not just about fun and games (although it *can* include recreation and entertainment). The "want" category is where your dreams are found. It is where your creativity thrives. It is where innovation takes place. These things will make the difference in your organization, setting it apart from others.

So, there are things that you *must* do, things that you *should* do and things that you *want* to do. Which of these three categories are most deserving of your time and space? Which is least deserving? Which should you avoid? In my opinion, you should avoid *none* of them; all are deserving. As we take charge of our time and space, I believe that we have to be working in all three categories on a consistent basis: must, should and want. If we do not, we will not be all that we could be. If we do, then this integrated approach to productivity will result in individual fulfillment as well as greater performance for the overall organization.

13. REST

Genesis tells us that God created the world in six days, and on the seventh day, *He* rested (Genesis 2:2). The seventh day was also designated as a time for *humans* to rest from their labors. In fact, we are commanded to rest.

Although I value rest, I must admit that this discipline is something I am still working on. Both my wife and my adult children have to remind me occasionally to stop working. Sometimes it is the Holy Spirit who calls me to a halt, saying, "It is time for you to close that laptop. Spend time with your family." Or He may say, "Take this time to pray. Come into my presence." When I notice that the Holy Spirit is talking, I do my best to promptly respond and comply.

The Issue of Laziness

If you are inclined to be lazy, this teaching is not an excuse for laziness. As I am giving instruction on rest, I am assuming that I am addressing people who want to be productive. If you are a lazy person, I encourage you to spend about three months meditating on the Proverbs. As you read those words of wisdom, ask the Holy Spirit to instruct you and to draw you out of your slothfulness. A renewed mind will lead to a transformed life.

Rest as a Scheduled Discipline

A lot of us need some practical discipline regarding rest. We need to schedule it, and we need to stick to that schedule. Yes, we should respond to the Holy Spirit's call to draw aside, but should He have to tell us to do what God's Word has already commanded?

Recently one of my daughters introduced me to the Pomodoro Technique for the management of work. With this approach, after every twenty-five minutes of work, I take a five-minute break. Then after four of these twenty-five-minute cycles, I take a longer break. Some have reported a three-hundred percent increase in productivity using this approach. The disciplined insertion of rest at intervals throughout the day improves productivity.

Rest as an Expression of Trust

Rest is important, because not only are we personally revitalized when we rest, but it is also an expression of trust in God. When you are resting, you are trusting that He has matters in hand—even though you know the project you have been working on is not finished, and you have a deadline in front of you. There are times you have to burn the midnight oil and just get it done. I get it, but you do not always have to work twenty-four-seven. When you take the time to rest, you are trusting the Lord with unfinished aspects of the work.

Even when I am sleeping, I can trust that God is still working. He even works in my dreams. On occasion, He has guided me prophetically through dreams, but even if I cannot remember what I have dreamed, constructive connections are being made between thoughts and memories. It is just the way the Creator has designed the brain. While you are sleeping, the brain is subconsciously working to develop solutions. That is why sometimes you can wake up in the morning and your waking thought might be a solution to a problem you have been wrestling with. Have you ever had that happen? It has happened to me many times. I have awakened and thought, "Now I know what to do!" That is what rest can do for you.

I have even seen the Lord eliminate items from my to-do list while I was resting! How is that possible? *He* has ministered help to people before I could get to them. He has resolved administrative issues and financial dilemmas without me having to lift a finger. He has laid it on someone else's heart to do part of what I was going to do. If you are diligent in your work, often the Lord will see to the things that you seemingly cannot complete.

Again, none of this should be taken as a license to neglect responsibilities. It is going to require some discernment on your part to know when to rest and when to work, but for the kind of person who is likely to read this book, the more challenging task will be to enter into this discipline and grace called "rest."

14. GET IT DONE

Admittedly, I tend to be a hyper-perfectionist as far as my own work is concerned. I think that I am somewhat gracious regarding the work of others, but I tend to be hard on myself. Aiming for excellence is commendable, but excellence and perfection are not the same thing.

Not long ago my son-in-law saw me overworking a project. I wanted to get every detail right, and after getting it right, I still wanted to make it better. Like I said, I tend to be a hyper-perfectionist. That is why in some organizations I've served, they like to assign projects to me that require great attention to detail. They know that I will do it right. Well, that sounds good, but a perfectionist can stall projects, preventing them from crossing the finish line in a timely manner.

So, here was my son-in-law watching me overwork a project. His current vocational field is in the area of marketing and productivity, so, he does know how efficient and effective systems should function. He said to me, "Maybe you just need to be done with that. You know, *done* is better than perfect." Now, that is the adage I want you to remember: "Done is better than perfect." As usual, my son-in-law's brilliance came shining through.

Before you run too fast with this concept, allow me to qualify it a bit. There are *some* endeavors in which being nearly perfect is required. If you are a brain surgeon, I want you to be perfect in your craft. I don't want a brain surgeon looking into my brain saying, "Well, let's just get this done." That is not the time to just hurry through a task. However, not everything requires the same level of perfection.

Be discerning. Know when a task would be just as good done as it would be if accomplished with perfection. That judgment call requires some maturity on your part, but both *done* and *perfect* can be expressions of excellence. Generally speaking, in most matters, done is better than perfect. [1]

---

[1] Sheryl Sandberg is generally credited with coining the adage, "Done is better than perfect."

15. MULTI-PURPOSE
YOUR PRODUCT OR SERVICE

Maximize the usefulness of whatever you produce. What do I mean by that? Typically, the work that we do produces something intended for use in one specific application, or it aims to satisfy one particular area of need. Consider the implications for productivity if the results of the same amount of labor could satisfy multiple applications and fulfill more than one need. I call this multi-purposing a product or service.

Allow me to illustrate. I am learning to multi-purpose the content that I produce. Let's consider how this book came into being. It started with a question raised by a college professor in a phone conversation, and that question led to an extended discussion, in which I highlighted some basic productivity concepts. Days later after reflecting on that conversation, I felt inspired to produce a spontaneous Facebook Live webcast. I sensed God's hand on that webcast, so, from the content of the production, I wrote a rough script for three episodes on my "Kingdom Conversations" podcast. While those episodes were being released, copies of the audio files were sent to a transcription service. The completed transcript that I received from the transcription service provided all I needed for the first draft of this book. While the book was still in production, major portions were integrated into an online Leadership Training Tracks course. Do you see what I have done? A webcast became a podcast which in turn became a book and then an online course! One product has been maximized or multi-purposed, being released and used in four applications.

Here is another example. Even now as I am preparing the final draft of this book, I am also preparing to teach an online seminary course entitled, "Church Administration and Leadership." Some of the material I am preparing for that course is going to also become useful as I prepare my "Kingdom Administration and Leadership" course for the Leadership Training Tracks platform. Additionally, I can almost guarantee that while I'm working on that material, it will influence my content creation for my "Kingdom Conversations" podcasts. Eventually, those audio files will be transcribed, and combined with other notes, all of that work will comprise the content for another book.

So, a person may look at all that I have just described and say, "Wow! In four months you have produced eight major projects!" No, in four months I have produced two major projects that have found eight distinctive avenues of expression and use. That is what I call multi-purposing or maximizing the usefulness of a product or service.

16. EMBRACE THE LAWS OF HARVEST

Embrace the laws or principles of harvest. I am talking about the metaphor of sowing, cultivating and reaping, which also relates to the cycle of summer, fall, winter and spring. Harvest is about a whole lot more than just reaping. There is a process involved. It is important to know what season you are in and where you are in the process.

Once again, I will use my own journey to illustrate. Recently I counted and came to realize that over the past twelve years, I have published over twenty books, a handful of those being for other authors. People might look at all I have pumped out and say, "Dr. Turpin, how do you find time for all of this writing in the midst of your other responsibilities? You are putting out two or three books a year!"

Here is the secret. I have been sowing and cultivating those works that you see coming off the press for about twenty to thirty years. Some of those projects have been in various stages of research and writing over that entire span of time. Now, in this season of my life, with a little extra work, I am able to push them across the finish line. As far as my writing is concerned, I am now enjoying a harvest as a result of years of effort.

I have a book that is over four hundred pages long scheduled for release later this year—only a few months after releasing the one you are holding in your hand! How is that possible? Where have I found the time to write four hundred pages? I found the time over the past twenty years. That is how a lot of this kind of work gets done. There is a time to sow, there is a time to cultivate, and there is a time to reap.

Also, note that you can have multiple fields you are working at the same time. In some areas of my life, right now I am reaping an abundant harvest. I truly am, and I thank God for it. That has not come about overnight. I have sown, I have cultivated, and now I am reaping. There are other areas of my life where I am not reaping a harvest right now. I am still sowing and cultivating in those fields. I wish that it was a time for harvest in some of those areas, but that time is not here yet. Until the time for harvest comes, I continue to cultivate and water what has been planted, knowing that one day I will reap abundantly. Recognize and embrace the process of sowing, cultivating and reaping in multiple fields, and do not ever quit. Persevere. Keep at it. Ultimately you will reap the reward. Just don't give up.

17. Avoid Reverse Delegation

Avoid reverse delegation. This key especially applies to those of us who supervise other people. Reverse delegation is when tasks that were supposed to be delegated to others end up on *your* list of things to do. This back-flow of work can hinder the productivity and creativity of a team.

In the early years of my leadership journey, this reverse delegation thing was a problem. I would call a meeting to discuss a project, but when the meeting was adjourned and everybody had gone home, I would look down at my notes only to discover that my list of things to do had just increased. What had my meeting accomplished? In effect, we all had this big conversation, and everybody came up with all these great ideas of what I needed to do! I was left feeling that I should have never had that meeting! That is not the way it is supposed to work.

The purpose for having meetings is to collaboratively work as a team to identify needs, set goals and craft plans. Those plans have to include the assigning of action points to particular individuals. The meeting is not over until every person at that table knows what they need to do once they leave that meeting. If someone gets up to leave early, stop them, saying, "I know you have to leave, but before you go, do you know what your action points are?" Make sure everyone is clear on what they are supposed to be doing.

Before the next meeting convenes, follow up with those individuals to see how their work is progressing. Your role is to encourage, resource and support them as they work to discover solutions and achieve their goals. Resist the temptation to micromanage. I will say more about micromanaging in the next chapter.

So, do not let reverse delegation happen. If it does happen, it is more likely your fault than the group's fault. It is a facilitation and leadership issue. If meetings are conducted properly, your task list should actually be decreasing, not increasing.

18. DO NOT MICROMANAGE

Empower your team to do what they are trained and gifted to do, and do not micromanage them. You have carefully selected your team. You have worked with them and delegated responsibilities to them. You have commissioned them, empowered them and supported them. Having done all of this, if you now micromanage them, you will defeat all that you have accomplished.

Micromanaging is a good way to deflate people. Ongoing work in a micromanagement environment quenches creativity, diminishes the team's sense of worth and removes the motivation to contribute in any significant way to the organization. Their thought will be, "Ultimately my ideas won't matter, so why even try?"

Your team members do not need you dictating every detail of how they should be doing their job. I know that you probably feel that you can do the job better, but in most cases, you are wrong.

Let people do their work. If you assign a person one responsibility today, and that person wakes up tomorrow only to find that you have stepped around them and have already accomplished the task yourself, that person is not likely to want to get involved with you in the next project. If you keep doing it yourself, you will ultimately have no choice but to do it yourself. People with a potential for high productivity will not stay for long in a micromanagement culture.

It is better to give people the opportunity to fail. Now, that may seem like a strange thing to say, but we have got to learn to release them. Yes, we want to set people up for success, but the possibility of failure is a risk we must take. Let them give the work their best effort. If they make mistakes, guide and support them as they learn from their mistakes. I am not saying that we forget them or the projects we have released to them. Monitor and wisely coach your team as needed, but do not treat them as puppets.

When I let people do their work without interference, here is what I have found to be true. More often than not, they have within them gifts, skills and character qualities that surprise me. They often surpass my expectations. In fact, I launch into projects with them, expecting that God is going to work through them in amazing ways.

Have you carefully selected your team? If not, then that is a problem for another book to address. If you have carefully selected them, take the risk with them. Release them. Let them fulfill what God has given them to do.

19. PRECLUDE ESCALATION OF PROBLEMS

Preclude the escalation of problems and conflicts in your organization or network of relationships. As the adage goes, "An ounce of prevention is better than a pound of cure." You can preclude destructive escalation by cultivating a culture of honor, empowerment and grace within the organization.

Honor

If we are conducting ourselves according to honor, we will esteem the worth of every individual. When we function with honor, we do our best to make the problem about the problem and not about the person. Here is where we need to remember all that has already been said about elevating "people over paper"—esteeming the worth of your people above your concerns about the situation at hand. As a team, have a predetermined resolve to solve problems together.

Empowerment

Each team in your organization should feel empowered to solve its own problems. Generally, problems should be resolved within the smallest circle of people as possible and on the lowest level of authority as possible. On this point, I am not just talking about interpersonal conflict issues. I am referring to any area where a solution is needed. If you are the supervisor, not everything has to come to your desk. Encourage your personnel to solve problems among themselves. If they cannot resolve the issue among themselves, then they can take the matter up-line, but seldom should a problem ever have to go all the way to the top.

If a problem moves too swiftly to the top level of administration, it creates a number of additional issues. First, it has most likely become an unnecessary distraction to the organization. Second, in the case of interpersonal conflicts, it greatly reduces the likelihood that the people involved can "save face" in the eyes of executive leaders. Third, if top-level administrators allow the problem to become *their* issue, and if their solution does not work, the perception can be that the leaders at the top are contributing to the crisis. Fourth, if the matter has reached the top, the whole matter becomes exaggerated in the eyes of the beholder: "Wow. Look at that. That problem was so bad that the president of the company had to get involved." Empower your people to resolve their own issues.

Grace

Problems and conflicts present an opportunity for grace and understanding. I know that the expression is overused, but it still has a shade of truth: "Nobody is perfect." In a culture of grace, before we pick others apart, we are careful to acknowledge our own faults and our own need for grace. Do you remember Jesus' teaching about removing the plank from your own eye before you try to remove the splinter from your brother's eye? Try dealing with your own faults, and you will quickly recognize your great need for grace and mercy. With such humility on our part, we are more apt to provide an environment in which others can correct their errors and emerge with greater successes in days ahead.

There is a facet of grace that is all about understanding. When we function in grace, we want to understand what is really going on at the heart of troubling situations. Grace sees manifested problems and conflicts as helpful warnings, signaling that something is wrong or broken, and it needs attention. When viewed with eyes of grace, it does not make sense to ignore problems. Grace welcomes the indicator and responds in a way that brings resolution long before escalation can occur.

20. PLAN YOUR WORK

When one of my daughters saw that I was producing a book on productivity, she said, "Dad, the first thing I would say about you is that you are good at planning your work." Her comment prompted me to examine what it is I actually do that would create this perception.

I would agree that one of the keys to my own productivity is knowing how to plan my work. I have an intentional, multiple-step process I go through in planning.

First, I identify *needs* and the *callings* of God. Needs can be identified through observation and assessment, but I have to rely on more than needs alone because the list of needs can become overwhelming. That is where the "callings of God" come in. I ask, "What does God want to do in this situation?"

Second, I set *goals* based on those needs and callings. What would be the specific markers indicating to me that the need has been met and the call of God has been fulfilled? I usually write down *three* specific goals for each need or calling, and then I select one of those three as my top priority. Why *three* goals? If I start out trying to name *one* goal, my hyper-perfectionism kicks into gear, compelling me to come up with the one and only one perfect goal. It can be paralyzing. If I go after three goals, I trick my brain into thinking that I do not have to be perfect. I can afford to be *creative* for a few moments! I can be "perfect" *after* I have written down the three. This technique actually works.

When writing down goals, I make sure they are succinct, single-sentence statements. These goals are measurable with targeted completion dates assigned to each one. As stated, I make one of the three goals my priority. If I do not accomplish all three, at least, I will likely accomplish one.

Third, on the basis of my goals, I craft *plans*. Each goal will have its own plan. I am talking about a multiple-step, sequential plan. I usually try to limit my steps to three or four per plan. So, I have three goals, and for each of those goals, I have a three or four step plan.

In a written plan, I also identify needed resources and processes. What personnel will I need? What will be their responsibilities? Where will this work be conducted? How much money will be required? Would additional research data be helpful? Would input from peers and experts enhance this plan prior to its execution? How will I assess my progress in this plan, and what will be my process for revising the plan in light of needed adjustments?

Fourth, I *execute* the plan. The old adage is to "plan your work, and work your plan." Here is where I put my words into action; I actually do what I said I would do. I have the plan clearly established in my mind, and every day I do something to execute my plan and to work toward its fulfillment. Having someone to whom I am voluntarily accountable for daily execution helps to ensure my follow-through. In my case, after our morning prayer time, my wife and I discuss the actions that we intend to take for that day.

Fifth, I *celebrate* the completion of the project. If the project was a team endeavor, I find a way to affirm and reward everyone involved. But who has time for such frivolity? If a project has been completed, isn't it best to just ride the momentum and jump into the next big thing? Wrong. Too often project administrators do not take time for this part of the planning process. Why is this step resisted? For one thing, it does not have the appearance of "work," and it definitely has nothing to do with real planning, or does it? Actually, celebration helps to highlight the best aspects of the work so that those practices can be replicated in the next endeavor. In that sense, celebration does contribute to the next cycle of planning, and it obviously boosts the morale of the team as well.

Once a project has been completed and the celebration is over, it is time to assess the strengths and weaknesses of the work. How might the team continue to build on those strengths, and what areas of weakness need to be strengthened? In the next cycle of planning, assessment should inform the forward movement of the team. The great weakness I often see in organizations is their lack of assessment, and even with some organizations that do assess their work, they seldom do much with the findings. Implement a formal assessment procedure and document your findings. Then make sure that your findings actually inform your decision making.

21. ELIMINATE NONESSENTIALS

The path to productivity begins with defining the mission, project, outcome or task. Once the definition is clear, things nonessential to that defined endeavor are eliminated. Once nonessentials are out of the way, the automation of the remaining tasks and processes is initiated. Anything that cannot be automated is then released into the hands of others to perform. After possibilities for delegation and outsourcing are exhausted, whatever is left over, that is where I devote my time and energies. Well, at least, this is my preferred way to accomplish things. It's not entirely how it typically ends up happening, but I do keep aiming for it.

The approach I have just summarized is based on a four-phase productivity model created by Timothy Ferris, author of *The 4-Hour Workweek*. His model is represented by the acronym, DEAL:

- **D**efine
- **E**liminate
- **A**utomate
- **L**iberate

When I teach or write on this subject, I use the word "Release" instead of "Liberate" to represent the fourth component, but Ferris and I are still talking about the same thing: outsourcing and delegation. Thus, my version of the acronym is DEAR:

- **D**efine
- **E**liminate
- **A**utomate
- **R**elease

In this chapter, I am only giving emphasis to the elimination aspect of this approach.

After defining the mission, project, outcome or task, it is important to eliminate nonessentials before automating and releasing aspects of the work. Otherwise, you will find yourself automating and delegating things that are nonessential to the overall project. It would be a waste of time and resources. Like a film editor preparing a movie for the big screen, you may have to let a lot of *good* ideas fall to the editing floor in order to produce the *best* streamlined "story" or product—your defined outcome.

The elimination of nonessentials also includes eliminating distractions and potential intrusions into the work at hand. You will need to guard your schedule to prevent meetings unrelated to your project priorities from happening. You should also make necessary changes in your physical work environment to ensure that disruptions can be minimized. Sometimes the process of elimination even calls for removing or reassigning personnel who are not a good fit for the work at hand. As you might guess, this process is often difficult, because it involves tampering with areas of your network or organization that some hold to be sacred. Be careful in this process not to cut away something or someone that is potentially life-giving, and if the process involves removing team members, please do so in an honoring manner. Once you have completed the work of elimination, you will then be ready to address automation, delegation and outsourcing.[2]

---

[2] Portions of this chapter have been influenced by insights gained from Timothy Ferriss, *The 4-Hour Workweek: Escape 9-5, Live Anywhere, and Join the New Rich* (Harmony, 2009).

22. Automate Routines

Repeated routines should not be reinvented every time they are needed. If there are parts of your work that are routine, and those parts require the same three steps every time you take on those tasks, then develop some systems to get the job done. In other words, those aspects of the work should become somewhat automated. You do not need to reinvent the wheel every time you need a wheel.

When I am working on a new publishing project, I do not start from scratch trying to figure out how to help that author get his or her message out. I have systems in place. Here is how I have automated or systematized my publishing routines:

1. My services are summarized in a brochure. When new authors inquire about my services, I have already thought through and articulated my nine-phase process, so I give them my Declaration Press Publishing Services brochure. It typically takes less than a minute to respond to an email inquiry with the PDF brochure attached to my response. I also include an Author Questionnaire containing the questions I have to ask of every author. Even the brochure information and questionnaire *could* be facilitated through a website download and an online form, but I have chosen to not remove myself from personal interaction with potential authors at their point of introduction. I may more fully automate these functions in the future, but for now, this is the way I have chosen to conduct business.

2. Fees are calculated using standardized spreadsheet formulas. By entering information gleaned from the Author Questionnaire, within ten minutes I can tell prospective authors how much their project will cost them out-of-pocket.

3. Templates are used for documentation and correspondence. Based on the submitted information, in fifteen minutes a formal Publishing Proposal can be produced, complete with royalty payment schedule and nearly anything else that authors might expect concerning their project. Once they sign the proposal, the same document becomes a Publishing Agreement.

4. Processes for editing, interior design and exterior design have been sequentially prearranged. Everyone on my publishing team is given a "heads up" concerning what I will need from them and when I need their portion of the project to be completed. Each project typically moves from one phase to the next with a great deal of predictability and few surprises.

5. Online distribution and sales are fully automated. With the exception of special purchases that authors may make, neither I nor my team have to personally be hands-on with online distribution and sales. Those processes are fully automated. Plus, "Print on Demand" technology has made the stocking of inventory unnecessary.

Once you have defined *your* project and eliminated the nonessential elements, what aspects of the work can you automate? Consider using email autoresponders, automated phone-answering menus and online appointment scheduling services. Refresh yourself or someone on your team in the full use of Excel or its equivalent as a spreadsheet solution. You can do amazing things with those spreadsheet formulas! Develop a procedures manual to guide you and your team through streamlined steps and systems for the execution of routine tasks and processes. Through the working of systems and the use of automation, you can greatly reduce the time that it takes to complete a project. [3]

---

[3] Portions of this chapter have been influenced by insights gained from Timothy Ferriss, *The 4-Hour Workweek: Escape 9-5, Live Anywhere, and Join the New Rich* (Harmony, 2009).

23. DELEGATE AND OUTSOURCE

After you have defined your work, eliminated the nonessentials, and automated routine processes, what remains? This is the point where you identify parts of the work that can be delegated to others or outsourced. You should not have to personally handle every remaining aspect of your projects. Release whatever you can.

Now, there will be parts of some projects you will have to keep your hand on. You may have to be the project manager, making sure that automation is running as it should, and making sure that delegated and outsourced tasks are actually being accomplished. You may have to be "quality control," until you feel confident that someone else is competent to steward your values and sense of excellence. However, do not micromanage. Your creative and visionary energies are needed elsewhere in the forward movement of your organization.

Once again, I will illustrate by providing an inside glimpse of my publishing business. One of the reasons I am able to produce so many books is that my hands are *not* on everything. After eliminating nonessentials and automating routines, I delegate and outsource. Someone else does the proofreading. I have copyeditors I can call upon to do the editing. I call on graphic designers to prepare book covers. I do not personally print and distribute the books; I outsource this work to third-party companies. I do not do all the work myself.

Define, eliminate, automate and release. These four steps help me to greatly increase my productivity and effectiveness. What aspects of *your* work might you be able to release to others?[4]

---

[4] Portions of this chapter have been influenced by insights gained from Timothy Ferriss, *The 4-Hour Workweek: Escape 9-5, Live Anywhere, and Join the New Rich* (Harmony, 2009).

24. BE RESPONSIBLY GENEROUS

L ife is like a river. A river has vitality because it is flowing. As soon as water moves downstream, more water from upstream flows in to take its place. So it is with life. As we give of ourselves, if done so responsibly, we are typically renewed and refreshed as the result of our generosity.

Thus, a key to productivity is to be responsibly generous with your time, talent and treasure. Jesus taught, "Give, and it shall be given to you" (Luke 6:38, KJV). I would go so far as to say that the surest way to keep or even increase anything in God's kingdom is to give it away. When I extravagantly express compassion or love to someone, my capacity to love is not depleted; it grows. When I give of my time, I seem to have more time for myself. When I give of my money in one area, more money seems to show up in other areas. When I selflessly share my ideas and insights for the benefit of others, more wisdom comes breaking into my thinking. You can see why I enjoy being generous.

As important as it is to be generous, do not allow others to hijack your time, talent or treasure. In the church ministry world, I would add, do not allow others to hijack your gifting or anointing. You are a steward of these things. You are not the owner. Our heavenly Father is the Lord of your time, talent, gifting, treasure and anointing. Your responsibility is to do what *He* wants you to do with all of this.

When others want to tag along with you or benefit from your success without paying the price, make sure that you have Father's permission before allowing them to do so. If you unwisely allow others on board with you, you run the risk of them controlling operations and shifting the focus away from your God-given mission. Soon such people can become unnecessarily burdensome, and they can seriously stall progress.

You may be wondering, "Why would anyone ever want to hijack anything I am doing?" Believe me, when people see that you are highly productive or have become successful, they will be lining up to connect their project, product or cause with the favor that is on you. Now, extending your favor to others is generally a good thing to do, but you do have to be mindful of this hijacking issue. The chapter entitled, "Define and Enforce Boundaries," is relevant here. You may want to go back and review that section again.

Sometimes it is with sincerity that people want to ride on the momentum you have generated. They may be thinking, "Wow, this is a very productive person. Perhaps with his or her help, I can become productive too." There is a legitimate time and place for that to happen, and I encourage you to wisely seek out opportunities to help others grow, elevate and move forward in their own productivity. Be responsibly generous, but do not allow anyone to hijack your gifting with a competing agenda. Do not be ruled by priorities that are not your priorities. Be discerning and responsible in your generosity.

25. LIVE IN YOUR SWEET SPOT

A im to live in your sweet spot. What is a sweet spot? I am talking about functioning in that place where you are saying, "I was made for this!" Allow me to illustrate with three intersecting circles.

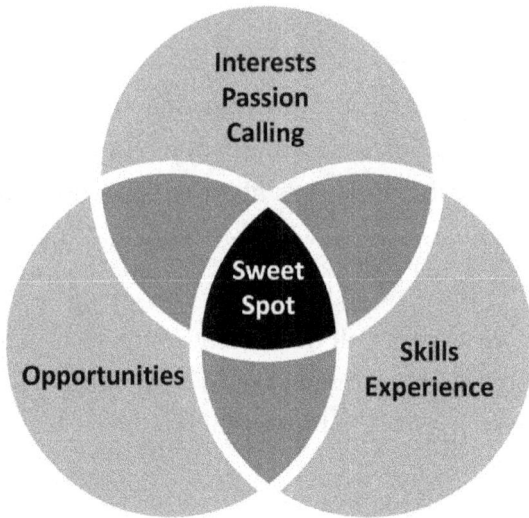

Interests
Passion
Calling

Sweet
Spot

Opportunities

Skills
Experience

The first circle represents my *interests, passion and calling*. If time and money were no object, I would give myself fully to this circle.

Intersecting with the first circle is a second. This second circle represents my *skills and experience*. I have acquired skills over the years. I have gifts and talents. I have experience and expertise. There may be some skills, gifts, talents and areas of experience I have that are not in my area of passion, but there is also an overlapping area where certain skills, gifts, talents and areas of experience *do* align with my interests, passion and calling.

There is yet a third circle, and this one intersects and overlaps the other two. This third circle represents *opportunities*. Take a look back at the diagram, and you will notice that with the addition of this third circle, an area has been created in the center where all three circles overlap. This center area is what I am calling my *"sweet spot."*

I do not always have the opportunity to do some of the things that I am both passionate about and skilled or experienced in, but sometimes I do! What a blessing it is when my passion and skills align with an opportunity! It is even better when that opportunity has compensation attached to it.

That area where all three circles intersect, that is your sweet spot. Aim to live there. If you cannot live there today, make it a life goal to get there.

26. FOLLOW FAVOR

When favor is manifested in your life, know this: *it is a great gift*. Take note of what is going well in your life in the areas of relationships, resources, opportunities and spheres of influence, and maximize that favor. Follow the favor you have been given in these realms as far as it will take you. Stated another way, be a good *steward* of relationships, resources, opportunities and influence. I learned the underlying concept for this key from my friend, Mitchell Corder, who is an uncommon, empowering leader in the Church of God denomination.[5]

Relationships

I have tried to follow this principle by taking the steps or actions that are clearly marked out in front of me. What is the next obvious step to take in that new *relationship*? Is a letter, email or greeting card in order? Is a meeting in order? How should I be praying for that person? Is there something I can do to improve the

---

[5] Bishop Mitchell Corder has served as an empowering church planter, pastor and administrative bishop for the Church of God (Cleveland, Tennessee) for over thirty years.

quality of that person's life or pursuits? Have they offered some service to me that I should be accepting?

While seeking to take steps with new relationships, do not ignore or neglect the relationships you have already been given. Begin with your friends and your own household—your spouse, your children, your parents or your siblings.

Resources

What is the next obvious step to take with the *resources* I have been given? Is there a tithe to be paid to the church out of those resources? How should I utilize those resources for the benefit of business, ministry or my family? What should be saved or invested? What should be given away?

Opportunities

What is the next obvious step to take with the *opportunities* I have been given? How am I to discern which opportunities to take? How am I to prioritize those opportunities? Am I to bring others along with me to also benefit from these opportunities?

Spheres of Influence

How can I best steward the *influence* that I have gained? First, I must identify the spheres of influence where I have favor. Perhaps you can relate to the following spheres, or rework these categories in a way that is more familiar to your context:

1. **Internal Influence.** I have been given favor within my organization. If I follow favor here with the heart of a servant and steward it

wisely, God may expand my influence beyond this level.

2. **Local Influence.** I have been given favor in the community or within the immediate reach of my organization. Faithfulness here may introduce additional openings to impact people, organizations and society on a broader scale.

3. **Regional Influence.** I have been given favor beyond my local community or beyond the immediate reach of my organization. My persistent following of favor within this realm may lead to God being glorified through my works on a national level.

4. **National Influence.** I have been given favor on a national level. I have favor with other organizations and national leaders. Although my influence may never expand beyond this sphere, I will not exclude the possibility that favor will take me further. I will steward favor wisely at all levels, and I will trust God with the results. (In ministry leadership, this National level could include denominational or trans-denominational influence.)

5. **Global Influence.** I have been given favor beyond national borders. I have favor with international organizations. Here I am positioned to inspire others to be a redemptive presence in all spheres of influence.

Once I have identified my spheres of influence, I can prioritize my projects, giving greater attention to matters that will yield the furthest-reaching results. For instance, if I have a choice between devoting three days to a project in the Local Influence sphere or devoting six days to a project in the National Influence sphere, unless divine wisdom dictates otherwise, I will probably choose the National Influence item. By making that choice, it is likely that I will accomplish more of what matters, in light of the far-reaching potential of those efforts. Also consider this principle: faithfulness in one level of influence often leads to influence at a higher level.

Share the Favor

Bill Johnson teaches that divine favor causes us to rise to the top in our area of influence. He also teaches that as we rise in favor, we should make sure that the people around us rise with us in that favor. In other words, share the favor. What I have already said about generosity applies here.

As we wisely steward the favor God gives to us, that act of stewardship often leads us to the fulfillment of our passion, interests, calling and skills. In other words, stewardship of favor can lead us into our "sweet spot."

27. Tend to Your Own Heart

Tend to your own heart. The condition of your heart impacts all aspects of your life, including the work that you produce. Scripture says, "Above all else, guard your heart, for everything you do flows from it" (Proverbs 4:23, NIV). If everything I do flows like a river out of the headwaters of my heart, then the condition of those headwaters is critical. There can be no higher concern in this study.

To use a different metaphor, your heart is like an internal garden. In a garden, you are selective about the kind of plants you want to grow. You want them to flourish and bear fruit. To achieve these results, there are specific environmental conditions that have to be just right. You need the right amount of water and sunlight. You are guarded about what you allow into that garden. Some things are allowed in, but other things are forbidden. You are careful to remove weeds and certain insects that might interfere with the health of the plants. Similar care is required for your heart.

Whichever figure you prefer, the principles are the same. We are talking about our spiritual wellbeing and the state of the soul. What are we allowing through the gateways to our soul—our mind, will and emotions? Are we guarding what we see and hear? Are we selective and disciplined concerning the words on our lips and the thoughts that run through our minds? What are the attitudes that rule our lives? How do we handle criticism, and are we careful to not take offense? When we are offended, are we ready to forgive?

Most importantly, are we maintaining our relationship with God and availing ourselves to the means of grace He has given us: worship, prayer, rest, confession of sin, repentance, inner healing, meditation on His Word, communion with the Holy Spirit and Jesus-centered community. All of these are factors that positively affect the internal ecosystem of our lives.

Reference to a number of preferred heart-attitudes would be in order here, but one attitude that immediately comes to my mind is the *attitude of gratitude*. Aim to be grateful. Do not allow criticism and complaining in your life. As emphasized elsewhere in this book, stay on the positive side of things. Look for the good in every situation, and express your gratitude through words of thanksgiving.

Furthermore, let your meditation be upon truth and not upon the lies that the enemy tries to feed you. Recognize the lies of Satan, laugh at those lies, and replace those lies with truth. Truth is whatever *God* has to say about you and your situation. Cultivate a truth-oriented, victorious mindset by keeping declarations of truth on your tongue.

So, what does all of this heart-talk have to do with productivity? Go back to the Proverbs' imagery of the headwaters. The condition of the headwaters affects the quality of the river. The condition of the heart affects the quality of what we produce. A polluted heart will produce inferior works. A pure heart will produce works worthy of honor and praise.

28. LIVE BY FAITH

Scripture says that "the just shall live by faith." In fact, those words are stated four times (Habakkuk 2:4; Romans 1:17; Galatians 3:11; Hebrews 10:38). What this means is that faith is normative in the life of God's people. It is what governs their decisions and actions. It is the mode in which they constantly live. It is what gives believers full access to God and to all that He has provided. It is what enables us to press forward in the face of apparent impossibilities.

Belief

In one sense, faith is *belief*. Technically, the words "faith" and "belief" can even be used interchangeably; they are translated from the same Greek word. However, in the English language, we typically see a shade of difference between the two terms. In Greek, the context often suggests a distinction as well. Belief is an acceptance that something exists or that something is true.

Faith begins to some degree with belief—an intellectual alignment with what God has revealed concerning Himself and His ways. The Bible says that "he who comes to God must believe that He exists and that He is a rewarder of those who diligently seek Him"

(Hebrews 11:6, MEV). We believe that God exists, and we also believe that this statement is true: "He is a rewarder of those who diligently seek Him."

Scripture teaches that "faith comes by hearing, and hearing by the word of God" (Romans 10:17, MEV). Here the belief aspect of faith comes through. What have you heard? What has God spoken? Do you believe it? Are you aligning your thoughts, aspirations and plans with what He has said? Are you agreeing with Him? If so, you are believing. If so, you are setting yourself up for a life of faith.

Trust

Faith is *trust* in God. It is relying on Him. The first key presented in this book touched upon it: "Depend on God." We are talking about confidence in the One who is absolutely unshakeable and unchangeable. Even if *my* track record is one of failure, that is not God's track record. He has never failed. No matter what undertaking is before me, this unfailing God is in my life. He is always big enough, strong enough, powerful enough, loving enough, wise enough and sufficient enough to help me through any situation.

When I am living by faith, I am leaning on this God and all that He is. When a problem is bigger than I am, my God is bigger than my problem. When I am weak, He is strong. When my situation is impossible, He is the God of miracles. When I am confused and don't know what to do, He is my wisdom, and He is never perplexed. When my resources are exhausted, He remains the source of all that I need. I am relying on everything He has revealed concerning Himself and His ways. That is trust. That is faith.

Calculated Risks

A life of faith includes occasions when *calculated risks* must be taken. Bill Johnson and others have said that faith is spelled "R.I.S.K." In one sense, trusting in *God* is never a risk, for He is always faithful and true. But trusting that *a particular action* will produce a desirable result is another matter.

Because we don't always have absolute certainty regarding an anticipated outcome, faith is often a risk. Additionally, we may not be one hundred percent sure that an action we are about to take has been ordered of the Lord. In such situations, the risk factor is clearly present. Nevertheless, we continue to trust and know that God is with us, even if we make a mistake. From heaven's point of view, we are securely in His hand. From a human point of view, it is risky.

Now, allow me to insert a caution here. When I speak of taking calculated risks, I am *not* talking about taking risks that potentially endanger people. Neither am I suggesting that you place yourself in harm's way. In some rare and exceptional contexts, a person *may* risk sacrificing their own wellbeing in order to help others, but as far as my teaching here is concerned, that would be the exception and not the norm.

Breakthrough endeavors often call for the risky kind of faith. If you are going after productivity in kingdom purposes, somewhere along the way you will venture into realms that seem uncertain and unclear. You will risk exposure. You will risk the possibility of failure. You will risk looking like a fool. As you mature in faith, I believe you will discover that such risk-taking is worth it. Learn how to take those calculated risks. Some of the greater accomplishments I have made in life have been the result of stepping into the unknown.

Courage

Faith inspires *courage*. None of the apparent hindrances in my life stand a chance when I consider the One who is with me. My faith is in Him. Does the task before me have the appearance of being difficult or even impossible? If so, it does not matter. I can go after it with confidence and courage because my faith is in the Lord. Does the situation make me fearful? My fear doesn't matter; faith-inspired courage dictates my actions, not my fear. I dare not think of any endeavor beyond my capability. Through faith in God, I have been encouraged (meaning, "instilled with courage"), and I will take on the challenge, refusing to accept defeat as an outcome.

29. LEARN FROM FAILURES AND SUCCESSES

You have heard it said, "Learn from your failures," I am sure. But it is most helpful to learn from both your failures and successes. Failures reveal weaknesses and highlight the areas where development is needed. Successes reveal strengths and highlight what you already possess that can be used to build your future.

This key is a little tricky. Generally, I give more focus to building with my successes and strengths than I do to developing in my areas of failure and weakness. Yes, if a particular weakness hinders progress in an area of strength, I will do whatever I can do to remedy the situation. With self-discipline, some weaknesses can be corrected quickly. But rapidly achieving perfection in an area of *reoccurring failure* may be next to impossible. For those long-standing negative patterns, accountability and perseverance over an extended period of time is typically required. Now, don't get disheartened with what I am saying here. I am actually making a positive emphasis. For the moment, my point is this: too much attention given to weaknesses can be discouraging—even paralyzing.

Think about this. For any of us, our list of weaknesses is almost infinite. To itemize all that I cannot do and all that I do not possess would require a sheet of paper stretching from here to the planet Neptune. There are trillions of things that I cannot do with expertise. On the other hand, my list of strengths is a much shorter list, but those items are powerful and have the potential to reset the course of history!

No one should take any of this as an excuse for being irresponsible with failure. Fix whatever can be fixed. Set *a few* development goals in your areas of weakness, but do not make your list of failures your focal point. What you focus on will get magnified. Yes, address your significant weaknesses, but give your best energies to building with your strengths. A strength-oriented person will often destroy weaknesses without even giving weakness a thought.

30. MAKE LOVE
YOUR OPERATING SYSTEM

The most important program on a computer is its operating system. An operating system is a program that runs all other programs. It receives input, guides how that input is utilized, controls peripherals and sends output. More sophisticated systems are responsible for security, guarding against intrusion and policing the activity of other programs, ensuring that they work harmoniously and without conflict, not adversely affecting the overall environment.

Make love your operating system.[6] Let it run all other aspects of your life and work. Love can monitor input, guide how it is used, control peripheral matters and selectively determine output—that which is outwardly expressed and produced. When love is present, there is greater security for all who are involved. Love guards against intrusion, ensures harmony and works through adversity in a way that benefits the overall environment. Unlike computer systems, love never fails (1 Corinthians 13:8, MEV).

---

[6] In one of my conversations with Steve Chelette in 2017, he spoke of love as the believer's "operating system." I must credit Steve with the genesis of the concepts I am sharing here.

How does this love work in the realities of life and leadership? Simply stated, always do the loving thing. Love will guide your progress away from being self-serving. Loving God and loving people is not just something you do in church. It is a way of living that guides *all* that you pursue.

This final key provides a fitting way to conclude this study. I'll say it again: love never fails. If you love, and *your project* still fails, at least you have done the loving thing, and that is no small accomplishment. This is the path to accomplishing more of what really matters. Love really matters. Love leads the way to true success. It truly does.

DECLARATIONPRESS.COM
Books by Dr. Randy Turpin and other authors

RANDYTURPIN.NET
Ministry and leadership training services

MAIL@RANDYTURPIN.NET
Email address for scheduling
or requests for additional information